Four Seasons of Me
Cierrah Haynes

Purposefully Write Publishing, LLC

Dedication

I thank God for this gift. I thank God for pouring His love into my life and blessing me with the gift of writing. I dedicate this book to my family. To those who kept going higher even in their low moments. To those who kept looking up when they wanted to look down. I dedicate this book to you. One who keeps hanging on and reaching for your goals. Don't stop. Remember, it's only for a season

Baby, my baby

Brushing her soft black hair
as she cuddles on my chest.
Perfectly round rolls shaping
out her tiny little body. Ten
little toes and ten little
fingers.

Nail beds were so small not
even a magnifying glass
could find them. My milk
rested on her breath, her

burps joining our
conversation.
Baby, my baby.
How you, my baby, came to
be. If sleeping were a game,
she would always come in
1st place. The ends of her
mouth crack a smile as
angels tell her knock-knock
jokes in her sleep.
Oh, you sweet little girl.
I celebrated your arrival.

FOUR SEASONS OF ME

My heart ran in circles
because a new joy came. A
joy that couldn't be stolen
or distorted.
Baby, my baby.
Rosy strawberry cheeks,
sweeter than anything in the
world.
When you rested in your
first room, I became an
artist, decorating your
second one.

I wasn't sure if you'd like the
color pink, so instead, I gave
you pastel greens and
purples.
You in my tummy felt like a
mama kangaroo protecting
her young.
So I placed a roo in your
crib to keep you company.
My A'mare J..
You are my love.
Forever and always,

6

Mommy Roo.

Conditionally

The pain that I couldn't bear
to talk to.
The pain of thinking that
there was more to the walks
I took to the finish line.
The intensity I felt, knowing
there was someone else
telling him that he could be
theirs. There was something
conditional about this
arrangement.

No, jealousy or envy didn't sleep in my heart, nor did it ever climb through my window and tell me that it was over.

I never fantasized about myself and someone else when I cling to my love at night.

It was in her best interest to find her own. However, I couldn't let it go that easily.

9

Oh, but I thought they
would be happy together
since this is what he decided
to choose.
He chose this pathway,
instead of the one I waited
so patiently by.
As I crept around the corner
of the hallway, I saw them
both.
How lively he is.

He chuckles when he's in a
moment of joy. When he
smiles, I smile. Look at him
- the perfect couple.
She notices me.
She jumps out of his arms
and runs to me.
She licks my leg and I look
at him happily.
Now, I am glad to
announce that my man is
officially a dog lover.

Dear Mr. Future

My past called me yesterday.
Today is the present.
I continue to look at my
future, and there, I see you.
The way you hold me on
our night of celebration.
Becoming friends is how I
should have started it, but I
wanted to tell you that I said
yes without hesitation.

I remember when I cheered
you on and you smiled and
looked at me as if we were
the only two people in the
room.

There was nothing awkward
about how we stood there
locked into each other's
thoughts, hearts, and
futures. Cupcake stains at
the bakery where we could
have met is ideal, but

instead, I saw you lost

outside a coffee cafe.

I wasn't sure if you needed

help with directions, or if

God had just directed me to

the man, I'd one day think

about.

The man I'd one day lean on

and the man I'd one day

have a family with.

  Mr. Future.

FOUR SEASONS OF ME

Wherever you are, I think
about your day in and day
out.
I imagine how great our first
date together will be.
I think about whether you'll
smile at me as I tie my
shoes, hum a tune, or just
doze off as we wait for our
ice cream.

Something about you
makes me hopeful for the
future.
The butterflies I used to
have only matured into a
graceful blue bird.
I fly higher now.
When I am cold, I leave and
warm up to you.

December 3

There are moments when
you feel like you've done
enough.
There are also moments
where you wish you could
have done more.
I remind myself of all the
things He said I would, and
can do.
I remind myself that He is
here with me.

Why do I cheer and applaud
when my heart is not
cheerful?
What is causing this, a
feeling of uncertainty,
discouragement, jealousy
that's trying to take over?
It's not a competition, but
for some reason, I feel like
I'm losing. I thought about
cutting my hair again.

Then I remembered,
someone explained to me
that when a person cuts
their hair, it means they are
going through something.
Before the clippers separated
my hair from my head, I was
happy.
 I felt free.
Now, I feel like if I cut my
hair again, then it will be

true that I am going

through something.

God help me.

Grieving Love

It almost felt unreal when
my heart began to sink. A
heaviness came over me
when you started to speak.
I wasn't sure if it was true,
but for you it was.
We just started to love until
your love for me was
"done".
My heart shattered and
shattered.

The pieces only grew
smaller.
This grieving love turned to
dust; no matter
 how strong the wind was, it
didn't blow away.
Sinking.
Deeper and deeper and
deeper.
The dark shadows turned
into faces that I recognized
and conversed with.

It was possible for it to
overflow, but I was careful
to not let it be so.
So, some of the hurt
evaporated in denial,
distraction, and distance.
I began to reappear into
society, reacting to posts
and posting myself.
But behind that post was a
heart needing healing and
peace.

Peace by piece.

Piece by peace.

Piece by piece.

His peace. Not his peace.

God watched me, as I

looked into the mirror and

repeatedly said,

"It's okay. You're okay."

It's going to be okay.

And it is.

Okay, it will.

His Daughter

His daughter sat well.
High shoulders, plump
breasts, and her short-cut
hairstyle with one size
freshly buzzed.
Lips cracked, but she always
came prepared with her
coconut mint flavored lip
balm.

One eye wasn't stronger
than the other, so her lazy
eye was noticeable.
She wore braces only for the
top row of her teeth.
Blue is her favorite color.
She's not older than 24.
She's not younger than 18.
She hid her age from the
men that preyed on her
looks and intelligence.
She wasn't promiscuous.

She, however, admired the
development of her body.
Shorter tops.
Tighter skirts.
Appearance meant
expression in her eyes.
She believed in expressing
her freedom through less
fabric and showing off her
cleavage and the majority of
her body.

Cat calling, offering up their phone numbers, sexual advances, etc.
These advances became a regular pattern she experienced.
Did she mind? Of course not.
Motivated by the attention she received, she continued to give more than she could actually handle.

It wasn't until she sat in her room when she noticed the amount of "fame" and "love" she was getting on her social platforms did not sit well with her.

Every provocative photo, every mini-skirt, and every crop top she wore, made her feel good, but deep down there was still pain.

It still hurts.

29

No, she wasn't sexually abused or unloved by her parents.

Then what was it?

Was it a little girl who wanted friends, but because of her appearance before, she never had any?

Was it a little girl who had loving parents, but due to their busy schedules, they

justified not making time to
spend with her?
Could this have caused her
to feel rejected and
forsaken?
Maybe so.

Katie

Two ponytails and a side
braid looked nice yesterday.
Today, I chose bantu knots.
I colored each knot with
golden glitter and decorated
them with shiny gems.
Cherry red shoelaces that
went up to my kneecaps and
a white t-shirt size XL.
I wore my little sister's
shorts because they had an

orange kitten on the left
back pocket.
I just bought these roller
skates a week ago and today
I felt like soaring in them.
Headphones in my ears and
my strawberry shortcake
popsicle liquefying as the
sun breathes on it.
Jazz and RnB did the tango
in my ears.
My long brown legs.

Stopping cars and creating
traffic is what I did.
Bop. Bop. Bop.
These tunes are so hip that
my hips are moving side to
side. Dancing with a partner
would be good right now,
but he wouldn't be able to
keep up!
Owe! This song is my jam!
Okay, Katie. Calm down.
No! I can't. This is my song!

34

Skating faster and faster, at
the same tempo as the song,
the wheels on the skates
started to loosen up.
Bad news. Terrible vibes.
One wheel pops off.
I'm flying. Painfully.
Thankfully, I landed in a pile
of leaves.
Thank God no neighbors
were outside.

Great. A bloody leg and
now a stained shirt.
It was totally worth it!
MY song was playing!

Lovely

As we ran through the damp
sheets.
You gently grabbed my
hand and pulled me into
security.
The smell of honey, white
lilies, and lavenders filled the
fabrics that we playfully
hung up on the line.

The sun bounced off of you
and blinded my love for
you.
Where did it all go?
The love.
It was so lovely…
I don't fault you, because
the sun saw it coming first.
There is nothing new under
the sun.
Something new, but this
isn't the first one.

Morning Drop

Wrapped in his arms after a
long day of listening to my
stories about my infamous
boss.
Coffee cup in one hand and
the other caressing my head.
Two teaspoons of organic
sugar kissing my ear.
His minty breath told me,
"It's always a beautiful
morning when I see you."

Today was the day I felt the
world stop. Taking me back
to the moment when I
didn't have to double-check
my phone to see if he read
my message or if it was
delivered.
My morning drop.
White sheets and four
pillows; none in the middle
interrupting his arms around
me, and no alarms

reminding us that today is
an important day.
My morning drop.
He wanted to break our
embrace, but I couldn't let
him. If I did, I would go
back to that nervous young
black girl thinking the worst
about a man who would
give me the world. So, I let
him go.

Warmth danced on my head
as he opened the curtains,
and the sun greeted us to
this morning drop.
My smile loved every bit of
him.
My face would light up to
my morning drop.
The alarm sounded this
time.
It was time.
Noon

Butterflies were everywhere.
They were little ones, filling
my belly as my knees started
to feel like water balloons
ready to burst.
My sister looked at me with
tears forming in the corner
of her eyes.
Was I ready?
Of course, I was ready.

Moments like this were the
reason for my morning
drop.
*One fifty-nine in the
afternoon*
Our eyes were in love with
one another.
This beautiful man that
lights up the darkest room.
Hugging my pain and
singing to my anger - my
morning drop.

His hands.
Lord, his hands were so well
constructed that when they
looked rough, one touch of
them would smooth out the
hard edges of my day.
His laugh was like the birds
that would serenade the
early morning hours,
greeting the sun another
day.

*Two o'clock in the
afternoon*

"I do."

No Looking Back at the Stories You Told

I gave them my word.

Surprisingly, I believed it

more than they did.

Confidence was key until I

lost the keys.

Now, my confidence is

unlocked.

Leaving the "OPEN" sign lit

up.

I'm not afraid that my
words are tatted boldly on
my chest.
I am only concerned that its
ink might smear due to my
lack of, or uneasiness to
keep going.
No matter what type of
word I give,
I will do my best to keep the
keys close.

Other

People told me that beauty
is in the eye of the beholder.
Family told me that I can do
anything I put my mind to.
Friends encouraged me to
go for it; to never be afraid
of mistakes, but always be
fearless to not give up.
World stop.

The voices of advice would
barge in at my heart and
takeover my life.
Feeling like a person with
many choices of my own,
became a hard thing to do
since I followed the road of
opinions.
What stopped me from
becoming me?
The tender touch of a
chance of hope darkened

when doubt shined brighter
than before.
Moments away of seeing a
winning victory became a
dream when sleep took over
my passions and times of
making it happen.
Why couldn't it happen any
sooner?
What was taking so long for
me to see exactly what
stood in front of me?

Like a man proposing to the
woman he prayed would say
yes, as they lock lips and
announce the news to the
world.
I was not in love with my
life or the proposal of living
in my passion.
There was no depression or
anxiety.
Only confusion.

A blank mind with nothing
but why to fill it. Why did it
have to go this way?
Why did waiting make the
result better than me going
right into it?
Why ? Why? Why?

Outsider

Going to many places would
have been fun.
But I stood still.
I enjoyed the stale air and
the hot morning beam
when I came from under the
palm trees. Jemima is what I
called myself after searching
for something sweet to put
with my coconut.

I've lived in Montego Bay
for a few days, and I have
not thought about the next
destination to live in.
A month ago, I traveled to
China in search of fabric that
would make a perfect head-
wrap.
There were cremé-colored
swans that hid between the
pink lilies, which sat on top
of the green satin fabric. The

yellow and orange vines
danced on the purple satins.
I thought about how many
warm and cool colors I had
seen before I realized I could
never return.

Overqualified

They told me that if I just
finished school, I'd make it.
They told me that if I just
finished school, I'd make it.
I stated this twice because it
was a repeated statement I
continued to hear
throughout my adult years.
Appreciating the advice, it
only went so far until I
finished school, but for

some reason, I felt like I
didn't make it.

I made it with a degree, a
career, and a family home,
but that was it.

Pursuing a career in
photography meant that I
captured everything.

Yes, the camera only frames
some of the stories, but with
what I'd capture, I'd turn it
into a series.

Every photo was
overqualified.
There was too much lighting
in this one and too much
focus on that one.
Precision and photography
couldn't get along. Making
my "I made it!" into "let's
make it!"
Did I go into the wrong field
or was this field wrong for
me?

Different question, but same
thought.
One. Two. Three. Four.
Calming my anxiety was like
the wind reading the waves
to sleep.
Purples in her dress and
different shades of black in
his suits.
They weren't married, but
wow!

They looked like a Happy
Anniversary!
Labeling this picture as
overqualified meant that it
was too good to not keep.
So, I kept it.
I told them my camera
broke, and the picture was
never taken.
Heartbroken while holding
hands - cute.

I had this degree, this career,
and this family home.
I took a picture of all three -
I am overqualified.

Peace by Piece

His peace is all sufficient.
A peace that is full and not
in pieces.
Piece by piece, some here,
some there.
 His peace keeps joy full; and
grace light.
Piece by peace.
In every piece of ourselves,
His peace is there to fill it;
To sustain us.

To lead us to our purpose

and always back to Him.

In Jesus name,

Amen.

Reflection

Looking out the glass door,
I thought I could see
something.
I thought I could see
something other than
myself. I tried harder every
time, squinching my eyes
and pointing my nose
upwards.
Nothing.

The glass hid from me.
Breaking it would only
damage my image and cause
my hands to cry a staining
fear. The frosted surface
turned its back on me, and
that's when I could see my
reflection.
Big brown locs.
My lips were so plush; it
made my cheeks look like
marshmallows.

Baby blue nail polish and
candy-coated eyelashes.
Pineapple earrings and a
nose piercing.
Woah.
Almond eyes and brown
sugar eyebrows.
Mirror is this me, or is this
the image you want me to
see? I promise I won't hurt
you if you don't hurt me.

Tell me something, is this
what true beauty looks like,
or is true beauty what I
should feel on the inside?
Mirror turned its back on
me again, and there I went.
Asking it to turn to me, to
show me something more.
Looking out the glass door,
I knew I could feel
something.
It was me.

Hi beautiful, I was waiting for you.

Salt and Love

The mountains cried out to
the oceans.
Each current kissed the
beach, waiting to meet
again.
Crabs came up from the
bottom of the Earth to be
welcomed by the sun, then
went down another hole.
What was the matter with
the mountains?

They were not happy.
Whenever the ocean sat by
them, the mountains would
begin to cry.
"What happened
mountain?"

Secured

Nothing felt better than
hearing your voice tell me
everything would be okay.
You turned into a string,
and I kept you in my
pocket.
Dreaming of a time when I
puked on your shirt after
finding out that we were
becoming parents, and you

held my worries in your bear
hug.
Married by choice and
parents for life showed us to
be workaholics in a matter
of months. I worked day
shifts, and you worked two
jobs.
Providing for us, for them,
even when you were
exhausted. That's when I
realized that we used to eat

for two, but now it seemed
like we were eating for eight.
Every other night our babies
asked daddy to take
mommy out for ice cream
and
Hot Cheetos. Daddy never
says no.
I feel so secure with you as I
carry our children, and as
you carry your family.

Sometimes I ask myself, how
could I have bagged such a
catch?
While those young kids are
out chasing a bag to secure
their life, you caught me
and secured mine.
My love, we are secure.
It's time to have a family.

September 20, 2020

There is no emptiness that I
would try to fill.
There is no lie, I try to say
that everything is fine.
I carry discernment that
comes from the Father.
In these past months, I've
felt like that person who
knows the truth, but would
rather stay distracted,

because it is safer and less
work is required.
Over and over again have I
thought about being so
bold in the Lord, really
doing the works of Him.
Why haven't I?
What is really stopping me
from doing so?
Today, September 20,
2020, God woke me up
around 2:00 am.

Is there something He needs
me to see? Need me to
hear?
I only want to live for God. I
just want to do things right
in His eyes.

Softly

The silky dress followed the
wind.
A quiet pink, that screamed
in the sun.
A heavy ruffle at the end of
the seams; it was the Queen
of its design.
The other ruffles served it so
faithfully that even the
crease knew when to
straighten out again.

The nude heels danced with
the pavement every time
they took a step.
There was such a rhythm.
A joyous sound came from
the store across the street.
Something they had never
seen before lighted their
eyes and opened their hearts
to be more giving.
They gave, just like she did.

A harmonious tune seized
the crowds and made
couples waltz on the
sidewalk. Ever so softly did
the woman with the silky
dress dance. She removed
her heels and began to spin
freely in the air.

Her orange and brunette
glistened as the sun poised
itself on the ends of each
piece of her hair. The elderly

clapped as she twirled in and
out of the heavy crowds,
children joined, and so did
furry friends.
Her laugh tickled the old
man with the sign. Her
piercing green eyes scanned
the mass and noticed the
amazement coming from an
infant. The crowd all
appeared to be in heavy
coats and jackets, but her

dancing brought them
warmth. Her smile was
contagious. The teenage girl
with angry eyes and hot
cocoa joined and began to
shed tears softly.
No, she wasn't sad. She was
at her peace.
The dancing woman softly
bowed because she fulfilled
her purpose.

Spring Braids

Rosemary drops to start the
day off.
Sunflowers smashed with
rose petals blended in, to
give scent and color.
The coconut and lavender in
the other bottle held their
shape.
Milk and honey stirred in
the bowl as the light-shined
through the window,

warming the mixture and
giving the kitchen a
signature aroma.
Carefully sectioning the hair
from the baby hair and
greasing the scalp.
Relief I felt as the grease
glided from one end to the
other on my head.
Medium-sized and
additional hair added.

The length of the natural
hair was ready for this
transformation.
It took a year and a half for
healthy growth.
This time around, it finally
arrived. Adding the bottle of
oils to the jar where the
sunflowers and rose petals
waited, for the start of
something new.

With sectioned pieces of
hair, the spring braids were
now beginning to form.
One strand under the other,
and the third strand waiting
its turn.
The smell of each braid
planted a seed into my
heart, turning me into a
flower child.
Finishing the style with my
baby hairs swooped and

sparkling dazzles decorating
each braid, took my breath
away.
Is she a model?
Possibly, but it's just me
with spring braids.

Stiletto

Business casual or dinner
party?
It's tough choosing when to
wear the appropriate heel to
an occasion.
Fancy isn't the word I'd
choose for someone like
me.
They look at me as a show
stopper, where they'd spend
their rent to put up with me.

Flattery is fitting when it's
your size.
I have trended multiple
times by your favorite
celebrities.
There is no need for me to
brag or boast.
Now, I am too CLASSY for
that!
My name is never the same.
Regardless, you know it's
me.

Too many trips make me
tired; so, they go out again
to buy me in the original
size and design.
My name is stamped on the
receipt, and tatted on my
face in our massive closet on
the glass shelf.
This is life.
She gave me one look and
got down to business.
Great choice.

Now, they'll see us from a mile away when I hit the streets.

Sunny Rain

Lattes and caramel candies.
Sitting by the window pane,
clear drops kissing the cold
glass, blocking its love for
me.
Hard thunders forcing the
walls to dance and the
chandeliers to twirl.
Children screaming in glee
as they parade in puddles

and play tag under the dark
clouds.
Wrapped in purple and
green polka dots, I watch as
they ignore the forecast, but
tend to their fun instead.
Where was my sunny rain
when I was younger?
I took cover in my mother's
comfort and hid between
the fluffy pillows.

Nothing amusing about
that.
I talked to my stuffed
animals and asked them how
could I make the rain go
away?
They only stared at me with
lifelessness in their eyes.
Tag.
He's it now.
I miss my sunny rain.

Super

Brown soft eyes
Mocha hair tied in a perfect,
sloppy bun.
Yellow squared glasses, worn
out denim jeans, and a
shallow green blazer.
My shirt reads: Smile
through your books and
laugh through your
creations.

I started to look through
the lesson plans and
questioned if they were
right.
I remember the first time
Principal Lance "jokingly"
said how teaching was only
for small women.
And I told him "I'm looking
to no man walking this
Earth for approval of what I
do".

Let's just say after that, he
began calling me super.

The Empty Bowl

I felt like an empty bowl.
A heavy emptiness that
never went away when filled
to the brim.
So full that you'd have to
walk carefully, or you would
spill some of me over.
My purpose was filled to the
top, but it would slowly
decrease every now and then

leaving me half-full or half-
empty.
A tiny hole at the bottom.
How did it get there?
Why was it there?
I continued to question how
this bowl, which could hold
many things, still felt empty,
out of place, and not
needed.
I wanted to shatter into
millions of pieces, leaving

the owner to cry, to regret,
to wish they had taken
better care of me.
But I knew that I was made
for a reason.
No more cracks, holes,
nothing that would cause
my purpose to leak out.
No more emptiness.
No more reasons to shatter
me.
I will only overflow.

I will become a greater bowl,

being filled with my calling,

my purpose - my destiny.

Thunder Boy

The sky was dark.
The tall grass covered the
ways of the fields.
Heavy winds zipped through
each strip of green life,
causing them to sway and
dance amongst each other.
A young boy raced with the
tall grass, running towards
the white moon.

He ran with speed in his feet
and determination in his
heart.
He looked into the endless
sky where only darkness
filled it.
Even though he couldn't
depict if he was going south
or west, he trusted that the
moon would lead him
home.

Barefoot with dark bronze
skin, complemented the
earth that he ran upon.
His dirtied tank top and red
shorts never defined who he
was - who he is.
This thunder boy of a child
was just like any child, only
this time he was different.
He had family and friends,
but no one ever saw them

because he kept them in his
heart.
No one ever knew his name
or where he came from.
The only thing the people
knew about this boy was his
speed.
He could outrun the
cheetahs that roamed freely
within where he lived.
At night, he'd lie side by
side with the elephants and

gazelles that were too afraid
of the stronger competition.
They called him Thunder
Boy because of his dark
complexion and because of
his speed.
Still, in the tall grass,
Thunder Boy began to lose
sight of the moon.
He knew that if the moon
was to go away, then, he

would be stranded, far away
from home.
He stopped running.
Suddenly, the dark sky
began to roar.
It roared so loud that miles
away, the king of the jungle
backed away and began to
bow before the sky.
Thunder Boy gazed upon
the sky and could see gray

clouds and stars form before
his eyes.
He smiled and began to run
again.
Joy filled his heart and his
belly.
He danced around the
grasses and hugged the air
because, he knew that he
had reached home.

Wilderness

Smoke darkened the air and
covered the sky.
Motion from the bushes
quieted her as she motioned
behind a thick tree.
She was not scared of the
animals that watched the
night.
They knew her.
Watching her take her first
steps on the earth, and

creating dances with her
older siblings.
They enjoyed the show and
she and her siblings
appreciated the
entertainment.
The young girl stood in
place, holding her breath as
the tiny creature submerged
from behind the bush.
Its spotted coat was so rich
in color

Tiny paws cracked the twigs
that lay beside the fire. The
creature didn't know if the
fire was safe.
Instead of taking his
chances, a larger
resemblance of him,
came from behind the bush,
changing his direction.
It swayed slowly; with its
chest sitting proud. The
young girl peeped from the

hut and saw the face of the
beast looking straight into
her.
She knew that if she ran, she
would be a meal within a
second.
So she stood there.
She made no sudden
movement that would
frighten the cub, and make
its mother threatened.

The young girl slowly
crouched onto the floor
into a position that signaled
the beast to position herself
also.

The cub was too busy
fondling pebbles and
fireflies, while its mother was
soon to approach the battle.

The young girl looked as if
she herself lived in the
wilderness.

Her hair stood tall.
Her frame covered with
brown cloth and leaves from
the branches that
surrounded her.
She and the beast circled
around the flames. The only
two things sounding off
noise was the cub and the
crackling fire.

The mother was focused on
her next supper and the girl
- her victory.
The young girl vowed to
never feast on animals who
were with their young.
Even though they never
showed this consideration
towards
 her family, she believed that
even with the different

beating hearts, they both
loved equally.
The mother began to charge
after the girl.
Screeches started to pour
out from the trees, causing
them both to hide for
safety.
Suddenly, the young girl's
father appeared with the rest
of their tribe ready to join
in and defend.

At that very moment, the
mother and her cub were
surrounded.
Double-edged spears
pointed in their direction,
making the mother and cub
terrified of their fate. The
young girl quickly broke
from the crowd; shielding
the beast.
The father was bewildered by
this behavior, but

commanded the spears to
retreat.
The mother and her cub
returned to the wilderness.

Young Man

My Mama always taught me
to be respectful to my
elders. I thought it had
something to do with them
dying soon since they
looked so old and skinny,
but Mama said that if I
respected my elders and
honored her and Pa, God
would let me live forever. I
asked God that if I lived

forever, would that mean
Ma, Pa, and everybody else
would die except for me?
God still hasn't answered me
yet. "Young Man. Where
you think you goin'?"
I told Mama I was heading
over to Sammy's house to
play. "Take these with you."
She handed me a pan of
butter biscuits for Ms.
Deeley. She was one mean

old lady. Ever since Mr.
Fred, her husband, died last
winter, she acted like a
lemon. "Hey there Young
Man."

I smiled and kissed her on
the cheek. "Sammy ain't
here. He went out to the
store with his Mama. So, it's
just you and me." I sat there
quietly and told her that
Mama made her some

butter biscuits. "Thank you, sugar."

We sat in silence for a while until she started talking.

"I know you think I'm mean,"

She was right.

"But I ain't. I miss my Fred."

"Every morning, Fred would get me a hot cup of Joe ready before he left for the shop; he would leave me a

plate of butter biscuits over
the fire. Once the Lord
called him home, I felt so
lonely."
I looked at her.
"Every time I see you come
with a pan of butter biscuits,
it reminds me of him.
You don't know it yet, but
you take care of me too."
"Young Man, you are going
to make the best husband

for your beautiful lady. You just wait and see." We sat on the porch, sharing a pan of butter biscuits.

About the Author

Ever since she was a little
girl, Cierrah Haynes has
always enjoyed writing and
creating colorful poems. In
moments of sadness, peace,
and sometimes doubt, she
knew it was only for a
season. As Cierrah uses her
God-ordained gift, she
knows that her family, her
friends, and her supporters
will be blessed in every
season they encounter.

126